Hollen Mead Barstow

One Evening long ago

Hollen Mead Barstow

One Evening long ago

ISBN/EAN: 9783742852106

Manufactured in Europe, USA, Canada, Australia, Japa

Cover: Foto ©Thomas Meinert / pixelio.de

Manufactured and distributed by brebook publishing software
(www.brebook.com)

Hollen Mead Barstow

One Evening long ago

One

 # Evening

Long Ago

One Evening Long Ago.

'Twas long ago, my children dear,
Occurred the tale I tell you here:
And on the old New England coast
Hard by the ocean's roar and foam—
A family group in an old-time home,
The children guests, the father host.

But who? And where? It matters not,
For women and men are soon forgot.
Too soon the hand of Time effaces
All that was dear and leaves but traces
For those who yet a little stay
And wait the close of life's brief day.

And yet oblivion is kind :
The skein of life will not unwind,

And strangers may not see the thread
That bound our lives with those now dead;
But 'in the Temple of the Heart
The fragrance sweet of Love remains
And lives of ours that formed a part
Still share our joys and salve our pains:
While to the world that heedless runs,
The Flood of Years still bears along
Upon its current grief and song
That swell the stream which makes at last
The boundless ocean of our Past,
And leaves but shadows for the mind,
Leaves but the whispering of the wind
That idly drifting may have known
Some part of life they deem their own!

———

The clouds all day had westward raced,
And as the gathering darkness fell,
The rising wind in gust and moan
Gave promise of the storm to come;
And overhead the shredded mist
Now here and there by sunlight kissed,
Drove by like silent speeding ghosts
From other lands and unknown coasts.

But not for long the strained suspense
While earth and air alike seemed tense,
For with a shriek and dash of rain
That smote the earth as with a flail
And made the old house groan again,
Rose on the night the southeast gale.

But while without was night and storm,
The cheerful fireplace blazed within,
And to the wind that shook the pane
And whirled around the outer door,
The chimney shot its shower of sparks
And answered with deep-throated roar.
But little heeded rain or wind
The group around the generous fire,
Who chatted in a merry way,
While from the driftwood high and higher
The flames of orange, green and blue
That many a flickering shadow threw,
Would leap and dance and then expire.

The picture comes like music's strain,
Till gathering mist is almost rain!
And yet of people plain I tell,
Not those who on the heights may dwell—

Not that rare group who at a time
By Longfellow told in charming rhyme,
Storm-bound met in a tavern old
Where each in turn their stories told
And made of their enforced stay
A long to-be-remembered day!
No brushwood hung above the door
Told passers-by of wine within,
And yet no vineyard ever bore
Such wine as flowed in Sudbury Inn!

And while the elders thought or spoke
Of memories the storm awoke,
Of ships at sea that helpless tossed,
Or those amid the breakers lost,
Some one who loved the legends old,
The rare old stories rarely told,
Besought the sister to begin
The well-worn Tales of a Wayside Inn.

And nothing loth for such good cheer,
Each listened with attentive ear
Till through her voice the poet's thought
On each its subtle charm had wrought,

And clear before us seemed to stand
The pictures from the Master's hand!
Out from the glowing pages stepped
Viking and knight who long had slept;
Again the old Colonial times
Depicted in the ringing rhymes
Seemed to have passed but yesterday,
And in our hearts we felt the thrill
Evoked by thoughts of Bunker Hill!
Then in the lull of the driving storm—
Aye, though the room was bright and warm,
Again we heard in startled fear
The midnight hoof-beats of Revere!

Then passing to an earlier time,
And people of a foreign clime,
Portrayed for us in flowing lines
The tales of which old legends tell—
That like the vintner's cobwebbed wines
Grown on his favored choicest vines,
Still hold the sunshine of the skies
And a bouquet that never dies!
Tales that were told ere we were born,
And will be told when we are gone.

And first of that Italian town—
The hamlet wears the poet's crown!
The Atrian bell whose ready tongue
Had long for right and justice swung,
But failing wrong and law's abuse
Had rusted from the long disuse
Until for lack of better food,
One suffering from ingratitude,
An humble beast turned out to die,
Espied the rope with creepers twined,
And having in a manner dined—
For off the cord he took his fill,
Pulled at it with a right good will,
Until the ringing loud and long
Brought to the spot a motley throng
Prompt to declare the steed was right,
And that his master though a knight
Be brought to book and made to know
The law reached high as well as low.

His wrongs were righted and the steed
Secured at once his·meal and meed
Of justice for his latter days
Without appeal or law's delays;
And King and subject both approved

The equity of a decree
That Justice still should blinded be,
And shield the humblest and the least
E'en though the suppliant were a beast!

——Of Scanderbeg who cleared the path
To power and fame of Amurath,
But in the shadow of the throne
Abandoned all to join his own;
To save from Turkish lust and greed
His native town of Ak-Hissar,
And in the dust and mire tread
The flag with Alban blood made red,
The flaunting Crescent and the Star.

——The cobbler of Hagenau,
Whose prudent simple-minded frau
Her passport for eternal rest
Had bargained at a monk's behest,
And with her treasures put away
The guerdon of a future day:
Regretful that her coarser half
Returned her faith with jeers and chaff,
And said her soul would drift away

Despite salvation bought for pay!
While soles he pegged, when he was through
Would last "until the trumpet blew!"
Content, because though purchased cheap,
Her days were easier and her sleep
No more disturbed by thoughts of death;
For lock and key secured the prize,
The certainty of Paradise
When she in time should yield her breath.

Then from the treasure house was drawn
A picture of the frozen North,
A tale from Scandinavian lore
Told in their sagas oft of yore,
And sung by scalds in Runic rhyme
As in another place and time
The minstrel Scot from door to door
Receiving alms and needed food—
To fill each heavy interlude
Sung Scottish glories o'er and o'er,
And for his eulogistic lays
Received unstinted, pence and praise.

———

But not for long the reader read

And pausing, mid the silence said,
"This night of all nights most befits
The reading of these charming rhymes
Of hardy sea-kings and their times,
For in the gale that roars without
I seem to hear the cry and shout
Of daring Norsemen on the sea,
And down the wind is borne to me
The hoarse halloo, the warning cry,
The 'ready about' and quick 'aye, aye,'
With surf or breakers under lee!"

A slender thread may serve to string,
A row of pearls to grace a king!
And thus the pearls of thought were strung
Along the lines of life he sung.

Then followed in a chatty strain,
That broke the spell as falling rain
The death-like quiet and sultry air
That fall before the tempest's blare,
Our comments wise and otherwise,
Our praises of the skill divine

By which the poet, line by line,
Had wrought with such consummate art,
And culling from each land a tone,
Created music all his own!

Then one who said he never dreamed—
To whom all things were what they seemed—
"The shadowy lands of old Romance
Are rich in deeds of love and daring,
And ready tongues bespeak the cause
Of those engaged in righteous wars;
While tales of beauty sore oppressed
Bring flushing cheek and heaving breast.
And when the poet tells the tale,
We find ourselves the dangers sharing,
And listening with bated breath
To see the hero win or fail—,
The lady rescued, or the knight
Victorious issue from the fight!
These ancient stories newly told,
Of maidens fair or vikings bold,
Are tributes to the poet's art
But scarcely seem of life a part.
Seen through a fog the keenest eyes

Behold all things increased in size;
And years are but a vale of mist,
The edges by Truth's sunlight kissed;
And when a thousand years of haze
Its pranks with human vision plays,
The listener finds ready tears,
And credence gives to all he hears.

    Yet after all is said and done,
The vikings of the olden time
Were nothing more than Goth or Hun —
The main distinction was in clime
A matter of mere latitude!
For might was right, and will was law,
And every hand good blood imbrued.
One race were robbers on the land,
The other of the sea and strand.
If Frank and Gaul in terror fled
At savage forays on their borders,
No less the humble fishing village
Became the scene of wreck and pillage
By Scandinavian marauders!

    But still the glamour makes the play,
No matter if that distant day
Was filled by deeds of piracy,

Or better still, knight errantry,
By doubt we lose, by faith we win,
And so I pray, again begin."

———

And then the reader read the lay
Beginning in old Stralsund bay
Of skipper bold, who by the cup
Put down his wine—his courage up,
And swore by Neptune and his spear
He never yet had felt a fear
Of spirits or Klaboterman,
And could he meet the Carmilhan,
The ghostly terror of the sea,
Would run her down—this valiant man,
And soundings find o'er " Chimneys Three."

No good e'er came of idle boast,
As found the skipper to his cost.
But bootless 'tis to here repeat
The stubborn Dane's foolhardy feat—
The thoughtless act that led to death,
But in the yielding of his breath
Gave him in lieu of stormy time
A quiet grave in an unknown sea,

Where spirits of wine nor men may be,
And the unfading crown of rhyme!
    For as the reader read, to me
This eerie story of the sea
Became as if an o'er true tale,
Not one derived from legends old
And to successive ages told,
But telling of the sob and wail
That drifted through our inky night
As if from witches in mad flight.

———

· As in the crystal of the seer
We look, half curious with fear,
The glowing coals now held for me
The stories garnered from the sea
By this old drift that as we spoke,
Its incense yielded in the smoke.
It even seemed as if the fire
Some spirit of the past contained,
And now upon its funeral pyre
With dying voice it low complained.

    And oft, I think, the driftwood fire,
If only we could understand,

Sings to us from the blazing pyre
Of moving scenes by flood and strand.
The Spirit, of the Sea within
The timbers broken, old and gray—
Poor relics of a bygone day,
Finds in the flames a kind release,
A haven at last of rest and peace.

———

The fire burned low, the flickering flame
Cast dancing shadows o'er the floor,
Around the walls and on the door
Through which securely fast in vain
The storm an entrance strove to gain.
And gazing on the embers dying,
There seemed to pass like shadows flying
Before my sight, the trials and fears
Of those upon the treacherous deep,
And those who watched in grief and tears
Till days and months grew into years,
And tear-dimmed eyes forgot to weep.

———

There drifted alone on a wide, wide sea,
With none to bear her company—

14

A type of deserted humanity,
    A broken hulk.

And deep lay mold and rust and grime,
And along her sides the slippery slime,
And the marks of the hungry tooth of Time
    All through her bulk.

Like a tramp of the sea she wandered alone,
Her home a memory, her name unknown,
No port that she could call her own,
    And no repose.

The rotting sails no sailors spread,
No sign nor sound of the lives long sped,
But fit to bear and be manned by the dead
    She fell and rose

Upon the slowly heaving swell,
The voice of her idly swinging bell
Mournfully tolling her funeral knell
    In blank despair.

The sport of every howling gale,

Only the faint and dismal wail
Of the slackened shrouds replied to the hail
        That spoke her fair.

O, the shapes that live in the depths of the sea,
Are reaching their thousand arms for thee,
And the sight is pitiful to me.

For once thou skimmed the seas as a bird,
And thy name with joy the mariners heard,
And at sight of thee their pulses stirred.

And dancing o'er the rippling blue,
The chorus from thy jovial crew
Flung back the cry of the weird sea-mew.

For thou in truth wast a gallant craft,
And came the gale abeam or abaft
The captain who loved thee only laughed.

And he pitied the folk who lived on land,
While he on thy yielding deck could stand
And guide thee with a single hand,

And list' as through thy rigging sings
The wind like a harp of a thousand strings,
While thy proud head the billow flings

As if thou scorned to be delayed,
And deigned not to feel afraid
Of shock or wreck by ocean made.

Now sea-birds perch on shroud and guy,
Or overhead with endless cry,
In swoop and circle tireless fly.

It matters not or good or ill
The measure of thy days shall fill,
For winds and waves may work their will.

O, type complete of hopeless woe!
That birds alone should see thee go
To thy home port in the depths below,

To settle in thy oozy bed,
Mid night unbroken and silence dread,
Until the sea gives up its dead!

Now ships from many a port are sailing,
　　To many a port afar;
And hopes are high,
　　And faith is strong,
But the last farewell is a tearful sigh,
For the way of the trackless waste is long;
And many have sailed
　　With a rising star,
But like the longed-for Ships of Spain
Are watched and waited for in vain!

———

O, the sea is patient, deep and wide,
And its depths a world of beauty hide;
And the beauty, wealth and power of man
　　It stealeth ever as it can!

———

A line of bay-indented shore—
The sound of voices through the roar
Of surf that breaks upon the beach
As if in vain it tried to reach
The boats and nets dragged safe and high
Below the homes that standing by
The waste of tossing, white-capped blue,
Are heaven for many a hardy crew.

Along the stretch of sandy beach
  I wander, careless, free,
And to the soul's imaginings,
The old-time sweet rememberings,
  Replies the murmuring sea.

Afar, beyond the watery rim
  The white sails melt away,
E'en as the twinkling lamps of night
That fade and die upon the sight,
  Before the dawning day.

And nature's quiet no sound disturbs,
  Or breaks the Sabbath air,
Save as the distant church bell tolled,
And called to worship as of old
  The muezzin called to prayer.

Cast at my feet a house of pearl,
  Untenanted at last,
Still holds the voices of the sea
And brings their whisperings to me—
  The echoes of the Past.

The mingled sounds of ages gone,
That haunt this fragile shell,
Are memories of those who sleep
In buried cities of the deep,
Of which old legends tell.

Like faintest hum of a city far,
The murmurings fall and rise,
An endless story of the past,
The secrets of an Empire vast,
And tears, and prayers and cries!

Again across the waters drift
Sweet airs that softly die,
Wafted from tropic islands fair
Where sea-maids sun their streaming hair
And sing their lullaby.

The song of the siren echoes yet
The charm it held of old
For old Ulysses homeward bound
Or Argonauts who dying found
The fruit and fleece of gold!

At times the music seems divine,
    For in the rise and fall,
And mellowed by the touch of time,
'The bells of lost Atlantis chime
    Beneath their emerald pall.

But still like thoughts between the lines
    I hear a minor tone,
The far, faint echoes of the cry
That hope despairing raised on high
    When Ocean claimed its own.

To me it tells of fisher-boats
    Whose haven once was here.
How in the break of day they sailed
Before the watching stars had paled,
    And sailed without a fear.

Into the break of day they sailed
    And met the rising sun.
But at its close they came not back—
The sea was strewn with floating wreck,
    And life and work were done.

And on the morrow laughed the sea,
   While women to and fro
In tears and cries upon the sands
To sea-ward stretched appealing hands,
   Sunk in the depths of woe!

Widowed and orphaned by the sea
   That lay so calm and fair!
'Tis fit the cruel deep should moan
And with its funeral airs atone
   For souls unshriven by prayer.

And ever the bell on distant buoy
   Tolls with the lifting surge,
Its monotone of dreary notes
That o'er the glassy surface floats
   The burden of a dirge

That Ocean sounds for those within
   Its caverns deep at rest.
No dangers fright, no cares may vex—
The oft-told tale of storm and wrecks
   Has ended every quest!

But the hours had sped
    The while I dreamed,
And the tall old-fashioned clock
    That long for kith and kin
Of mine had marked the hours,
With hands upright before its face
    Now told the morrow's birth:
And then with sweet and mellow stroke
    In tone of mild reproach,
Twelve times it slowly struck,
And each stroke plainly said
''Tis time that dreamers were in bed!'

And so the evening ended,
    And the time
You here have given to my rhyme
    Must likewise end:
And I perhaps, for undue length,
Should proffer my amende.

�֍ CHIPS. ✤

Hymn of the Sea.

O, list, my soul to the grand old hymn
   Intoned by the restless Sea
Since first to the hearts of men it brought
The grandeur that God hath wrought,
   And bringeth now to me.

The rolling boom of the distant surf
   In diapason deep,
Blends with the ripples on the shore
That rhythmic flow forevermore
   And lull to rest and sleep.

Like a minster organ's solemn tone
   The music fills the air
And rises to the vaulted blue
As rendering the homage due
   Him who abideth there.

And be the anthem deep and strong,
 Or soft like distant bell;
Blow southern breezes sweet and mild,
Or eastern gales so fierce and wild,
 Still shall the pæan swell.

For since the waste of waters felt
 The Spirit o'er them move
And heard the Word "Let there be Light"—
The Word that banished Endless Night,
 The sea has voiced His love,

And sounded ever to the High
 A glorious Hymn of Praise,
That rising since creation's morn
Will sound till Heaven on earth shall dawn,
 To Him, Ancient of Days!

And I Shall Not Forget.

A sweet refrain abides with me,
  The echo of a tender song
That filled my heart when life was free
  And love was sweet, and hope was strong;
And through the years 'tis sounding yet—
  The promise I have known so long—
    "And I Shall Not Forget."

'Twas sung in the glow of youth's bright morn
  By the shore of the whispering sea,
And I hear it still though the glow has gone,
  For the singer was all the world to me.
And it bides till the sun with me shall set
  And the loved and lost again I see—
    And I shall not forget.

27

For night came down with grief and the pall,
  And I hear that song on earth no more.
But clear it rings in the starry hall
  And adown an unseen Golden Shore.
And the promise given when here we met
  Shall be kept with me forevermore—
    And I shall not forget.

O, promise sweet that came with love,
  And lives when all of earth has gone!
The strain that falls from the stars above
  Will rise anew in the Risen Dawn.
And we shall meet as once we met
  When life and love were in their morn—
    And I shall not forget.

Eugene Field.

The Children's Poet is sleeping
    With the key to Childhood's Heart—
And stilled the hand and mind that wrought
    For them with loving art.

Yes, wrapped in sleep, but ever
    His dreams and fancies stay,
And long for children's hearts shall make
    A happy holiday.

Still as the Night-wind moans,
    Comes with a fear and start
The consciousness of " Who's been bad?"
    Within the childish heart.

And still the soldier waiteth
  The Little Boy Blue's command—
But father and child their dream-life live
  Where naught is but Dream-land.

Still on the "Dream-Ship" saileth
  Under the starry night—
Still at its side the angels stand—
  Three angels robed in white.

But now beside the Spirit
  That standeth "crowned with rue,"
Bright with a light divine appeareth
  The kindly face we knew.

Softly to earth there floateth
  From that familiar hand
Dreams that the old and young delighteth
  In every time and land!

November 15th, 1895.

The Fishing Fleet.

"Off for the Banks," the fishermen cry,
  And "off for the Banks" the fishwives sigh,
      For the days are long
      And the nights are drear,
And while they hearten their men with song,
  Their leaden hearts are filled with fear.

For they remember the season past,
  When a blinding gale and freezing blast
      Raged on the Banks
      All through the night,
And quietly out of the floating ranks
  Dropped many a fisherman's riding light.

And the struggling gray of the morrow's morn,
  Found half of the gallant vessels gone.
      - But the wind that blew,

Nor the sea that laughed,
Brought to the ear a hail from the crew,
Nor token showed of the missing craft.

And the boats that fled from the place accursed,
Sailed with their drooping flags reversed.
And women in tears
Adown the shore,
Read from afar of the coming years—
The tale the fluttering pennants bore.

And to those who wait and watch in vain,
Lover and husband come never again.
And the storm they hate,
And the sea they dread,
For the one has wrought them cruel fate,
And the one withholds their dead.

And this is the reason the fisherman's cry
Drags from their woman-kind a sigh.
And the old fish-wife
Croons her sad song—
"The sea is cruel and robs our life,
And nights are drear and days are long."

Day Dreams.

———

"We spoke of many a vanished scene,
　　Of what we once had thought and said,
Of what had been and might have been,
　　Of who was changed and who was dead."

　　—Longfellow, "The Driftwood Fire."

In dreams by day there comes to me
　　The face and scene of the long ago,
The home of my youth again I see—
　　The town so quiet and quaint below
The hills that overlook the bay—
　　The narrow streets through which I go
As when a boy, and that to-day
　　Run here and there from wood to sea,
And now as then to the childish mind
　　Are part of a strange weird mystery.
The mystery of by-gone years—
The story of loves and hopes and fears,
Of those who were but now are not,
Of those remembered, those forgot.

33

These very stones that bed the street
So unresponsive to the touch
Could they but speak, would say so much!
    For they had counted myriad feet
Before the field became a street!

———

The old home fronts upon the sea
    Scarce half a cable's length away;
And oft as a child it seemed to me
    They had their quiet, unnoted play;
For House and Sea are old, old friends
    And fleeting years have a century spanned
Since first by the favor friendship lends,
    The restless waves upon the strand
That slip ashore in rhythmic time
Light voyagers from some other clime,
Told it their weird or thrilling tale
Of vexing calms, or wreck and gale;
Of ships that gaily sailed from port
    And then returned to port no more!
But watched and waited for in vain
    Have left their bones on ocean's floor
Or rocky reefs across the main;
    Of shapes that fled before the storms

With rope untouched and canvas spread,
Manned by the silent ghostly forms
Their brother sailors deem as dead!
  Who, as they drive before the gale,
Return to cries no answering hail
But fly on their unending quest,
To others neither host nor guest!

And to the whispering summer sea,
    Or shriek of piercing wintry gale,
The House has listened eagerly
    And felt each cry, each sobbing wail;
And as it heard the saddened moan
    With echoes of the dying fraught,
Has answered with a creak and groan
    As if it shivered at the thought!

———

Where once the Indian's wigwam stood,
    The church and school stand side by side,
In the shadowy depths of the spreading wood
    The Narragansett wooed his bride.
From bay and shore he drew the store
    Made ready for his idle hand,
And needing less and finding more

He blessed the kind and fertile land,
And as for quiet and rest he came,
He gave the place its Indian name.*

A thousand ships have left these wharves
   For every port and clime:
Some have returned and others stayed,
Some in their ports will be delayed
   Unto the end of time!
The gray sea-beards that rise and fall
   Upon each stony face,
Declare the age of witnesses
That speak of long gone argosies
   And Ocean's rough embrace.

———

Like shadows from low-flying clouds
   The passing phantoms come and go,
Not singly, but in sweeping crowds—
   The shades of those I used to know.

Aye, used to know but know no more,
   For mile-stone years have come between
And point the way from shore to shore,
   From boyhood to the closing scene.

* "Mattapoisett." Signifying "Place of Rest."

The sighing pines their vigil keep,
      And stone and tablet mark the place
Where in their long and dreamless sleep
      They lie—the fallen in the race.

And still they moan the last requiem
      For those who sleep so sound below—
I hear the music in my dream
      In mournful cadence weird and low.

They whisper to the restless sea,
      And to the sailor on the main
Is borne the air from the distant lea
      In tender, low and sweet refrain.

The sea-gull's wing still flecks the blue
      And the flashing gleams of white
Shoot through the Summer air as do
      The star-beams through the mists of night.

The light-house, warder of the coast,
      Still throws its guiding beams abroad—
To many a sailor tempest tossed
      It seems a saving sign from God!

And woods and shore and wharf and weed
    Are redolent of years long fled;
Of passing man they take no heed,
    But breathe the story of the dead.

———

The pictures hang on Memory's wall,
    And none shall say me nay
That from the dim and distant past
Of which we form a part at last,
I draw from stores of treasures vast,
    And care not for To-Day.

To Richard Henry Stoddard.

_____

With deference but aye with love,
My heart its tribute sends,
And to the greeting I would add
The warmth that friendship lends.

So if among the laurel leaves
There grows no spray of pine,
I pray thee to accept as such
This halting verse of mine.

And when beside the western sea
My heart shall voice thy praise,
Thine may it reach like vesper chimes
In the Evening of thy Days!

39

Stoddard---At Seventy.

His is the seamy side of life,
And well he knows the care and strife
　　That vex the poor.
The human tide in restless sweep
Like waves and eddies of the deep,
　　Breaks at his door.

He dwells amid the life and jar,
Of busy men, but from afar
　　He draws his song
That swells beyond the city's bound,
Until the world has heard the sound
　　So true and strong.

The 'Songs of Summer' he may sing,
Of 'Bells' that only once may ring,
　　Or friends that part.
The note the soaring lark might trill—

Of mountain brook or purling rill
　　Flow from his heart.

　To gardens in far-off Cathay—
To deserts where the Nubians stay,
　　He leads the mind.
The Orient and the West are ours—
With him we linger 'mid the flowers,
　　Or ride the wind.

　And rising from that little room
The song is scented with the bloom
　　Of country highways.
Or with a deeper, tenderer strain
He speaks for one in shame and pain
　　In city by-ways.

　The anthem of the mighty Deep,
The yodel of the Alpine steep
　　Are sung by him.
What matter if the hair is gray,
Or twilight hastens after day,
　　Or sight is dim?

　Almost he sees that far-off coast,

And hears the sweetly choiring host
    That once he knew.
The poets who tarried on the earth
And gave to Song its newer birth,
    Await him too.

  For he has passed the scriptural bound,
And sits with bay and laurel crowned,
    Close by the Gate.
A creditor of human kind,
Infirm but brave, and weak and blind.
    And this is fate!

  Stoddard, one place is not for thee!
Thy home is every land and sea
    And every heart.
Each day some door shall open wide,
And there shalt thou in peace abide,
    Of Life a part.

  Each day some heart shall offer rest
And make of thee an honored guest
    For thy sweet song.
The monument built by thy hand,
That speaks for thee in every land,
    Endures for long!

The Fisher Boy.

[From Schiller's William Tell.]

The laughing Sea to its bosom wooes
    The boy asleep on the shore
And the dreaming child tired out by play
    Shall wake on earth no more.
Sweet music o'er his senses steals
    Like airs from Paradise,
Or flute-tones sweet or distant bell—
    In sleep he dreams—and dies!
The waves now playing about his breast
    Have claimed him for their own,
And from the erstwhile laughing Sea
    There comes in deeper tone
" Long have I loved thee, dearest boy,
    And now shalt thou be mine.
'Twas I that cradled thee in sleep,
    'Tis I who lovingly entwine!"

Im Frühlingseiten.

In the beauteous month of May,
    When buds and flowers start,
The Flower of Love renewed
    Blooms in my loving heart.

In the beauteous month of May,
    When singing birds are thronging,
I could but whisper thee
    My heart's sincerest longing.

For the Fly·Leaf·of the Rubaiyat.

The Seeker for the Light herein
These burning lines shall scan in vain.
   No Soul a recompense shall win
For Faith undimmed or earthly Pain.

No narrow Road ends at a Gate—
But Birth and Life and Life's long Sleeping
   Are written by a Hand of Fate
That heeds nor hears your Prayers nor Weeping.

Life's perfect round begins and ends
In Dust.   Our Hopes succeed or fail—
   The Arc attained our Chord subtends
The Hand drops down its Veil!

Auf Wiedersehen.

It is by God's decree appointed,
  That man from all he loves—
From all he loves or has, must part,
  And nothing in the world abides:
    The keenest grief of every heart
  Is parting pain.
Yet should we rightly understand
  The kindness of the law,
  For when we walk with lingering feet—
  When paths diverging bring but grief,
Heart cries to heart " Again we'll meet,
  Yes, meet again!"

www.ingramcontent.com/pod-product-compliance
Lightning Source LLC
Chambersburg PA
CBHW021546270326
41930CB00008B/1384